BUILDING
A NEST FROM
THE BONES
OF MY PEOPLE

Cara-Lyn Morgan

Invisible Publishing
Halifax & Toronto

Library and Archives Canada Cataloguing in Publication
Title: Building a nest from the bones of my people / Cara-Lyn Morgan.
Names: Morgan, Cara-Lyn, author.
Subjects: LCGFT: Poetry.
Identifiers: Canadiana 20230193277
       ISBN 9781778430305 (softcover)
       ISBN 9781778430312 (EPUB)

Classification: LCC PS8626.O7438 B85 2023 | DDC C811/.6—dc23

Edited by Adebe DeRango-Adem
Cover and interior design by Megan Fildes | Typeset in Laurentian
With thanks to type designer Rod McDonald

Invisible Publishing is committed to protecting our natural environment. As part of our efforts, both the cover and interior of this book are printed on acid-free 100% post-consumer recycled fibres.

Printed and bound in Canada.

Invisible Publishing | Halifax & Toronto
www.invisiblepublishing.com

Published with the generous assistance of the Canada Council for the Arts, the Ontario Arts Council, and the Government of Canada.

Canada Council
for the Arts

Conseil des Arts
du Canada

ONTARIO ARTS COUNCIL
CONSEIL DES ARTS DE L'ONTARIO
an Ontario government agency
un organisme du gouvernement de l'Ontario

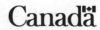

For my child, for my sisters
For all of us.

Words, scattered

dustbowls on this wide
and acred place. *Innocence,*
pureté, famille,
foi. Every night, I pluck
red and black feathers

from my wings until
I am flightless
and cold.

I dreamed
I tongued the ridge
of my gums and found my teeth

had fallen out, nested in
layers of star thistle,
poplar fluff

at the base of the gravel pit
we played in as girls. I found and
flattened them
on the railway line, cast
along the tracks to be pocketed
like pennies.

I dreamed I shed my fingernails
to their nervy beds, and spread
each along the fallow
so wildflowers
might spring up, bloody.

Loose

flutter of memory drifting
a voice through phone
and tequila,

touching memory
touching

twenty years separate us
yet   I remember

the ones we should not hug,
should never leave
with our children.

An uncle
gets drunk, tells
me he has known
both sides of this.

Later, calls me
an asshole.

I become the collector
of slurred and weeping
half-confessions,
fogged memories

touching memory
touching, denial.

They squat in
the back of my skull
I can't remember

how to breathe
to sleep, to remember.

One by one: named.
One by one: silenced.

An aunt tells me
it's something
that happens when you are a child
and you have to move on.

I am told
everyone should
just get over it. I am told
it'll all work out.

The ruiners

breakers
of rules. unlinkers
a very old chain. My sisters and I

ask each other
what do you remember?

Lights at night.

Stairs creak.
A whisper?

Nothing.

We remember
nothing.

Tangled sweetgrass

I count 21 and snip close to the white
the hair of our Mother. I will braid
in groups of seven. Put tobacco
in the earth. My feet
have been planted in this prickled ground
far too long. I have ashed

my skin in it
like a heated cow. This male
thirst—folding

table, smoky
living room. A game
of cards. Women thick-hipped
against the kitchen counter, arms
crossed over pregnant bellies.

Ten little girls
picnicking beneath
the card table, pretending
to drink tea, smoking
our Crayolas.

I did not know then
I was choking.

I am not orphaned

only loved
deeply

by the keepers
of the worst secrets.

Tiny

winged thing, neither bird
nor butterfly. Pixied and quiet
always a star. I can not name
the one who called

out the dead and all
of us living. This is my last
protection. She, a hummingbird's
breast, spot
on a monarch's
wing, the first shocking droplets
of womanhood.

The ghosts of our kin
awakening.

Break

the last of our dead
grandmother's champagne
flats. Sweep up the shards.

On a night soon after, she comes
to the room where you sleep,
touches the soft skin
of your upper arm. You
startle

awake to a dark, empty room. Tell
your husband and he falls back
asleep, laughing. Ghosts
are funny
to the unhaunted.

Break

ground, a perfect square. One
corner for each direction—a place
for all these ashes.

This eyeless doll

Kissed
to death, threads
unwound—
a frayed

and flattened thing. Slept with
too long, sweat-heavy, she stares
through unstrung eyes.

Played with
until her arms began
to separate beneath her
eyelet dress—

outgrown, then
cast aside.

This quieting

of lashes, loosening
of the muscles around
the eye. From here
on the 36th floor
I can hear a boy beating

a plastic tub, pounding rhythms
above traffic, above

the rising heat. My fiancé has left
himself to rest, a beer

warming in his big
and blistered hand. I alternate

between the view of all the things
I never cared for and him
still and sleeping finally,
the ring he slid
on my finger this morning
after a marathon
of bickering.

I am awake,
singing quietly.

Who kissed my bleeding parts

for Sean

I say, *I'm fine.*
I'm fine, I'm fine.

I am tangled
in quilts on the sofa,
rubbing tracks into the skin
from my neck. I have scratched
my skin bloody as long
as I can remember. Scratched

past blood until sticky gold
bubbles dotted my calves, ringed
hot and pink.

You kneel down, pull my hands
from my neck, breathe
long and loud
say *breathe*
breathe
breathe

say,
forget the past. It's only
us. I'm here, I'm here
I'm here.

Your t-shirt smells like concrete dust
and sweat.

When we sleep,
you catch my relentless hands, hold
my fists before I can start. Press

my shortened nails to your own chest
and tell me to scratch your skin
instead.

How often were we held

above the heads
of black-haired men. How freely

our skirts bloomed, knee socks
crumpled around narrow calves. How
much did we know. How little.

This cankers
my tongue: that I know

I have slept among
the ruined.

My biggest fear

is to be
someone's wife. I do not wish
to clean the socks of someone
else. To defer the remote. To rush
my shopping because you opted to wait
in the hot parking lot rather than to let me
drive myself. I do not wish to be criticized. Nights

leading up to the wedding
I have forgotten to breathe,
burst into tears,
drank too much. Today

my near-husband is likely
just waking, with a happy hangover
in a separate hotel across the way.
I have known

my entire life
I will be no good.

Two AM

An orange streetlight bounces
off the stainless fridge, spills back
through the open bedroom door. Beside me,

this man I married sleeps
and I am jealous. We do not yet know
we will be parents soon. Usually
it is he who flicks in and out of the sheets,
pummeling pillows from cases, flopping
from broad shoulder to back, huffing.

Lately, though, I am the one
with eyes restless in the black. I have begun
scratching my calves again, bloody. Each night
I starve myself nauseous and then stare
into the toilet water, resisting my fingers
into my throat for relief.

I have never known
silence in prayer. I am
unanswered.

Hummingbird

She closes her eyes, slows
her heart, bones draped on ridges of bone. On her
side, she rests her breast against the shell of her wing. Talons
grip at air. She comes to slumber, crust of stamen
on her tongue. She,

a thing of silent, startling scarlet. Appearing always in the breath
of sky, amongst a wave of heat and grapevine. Tonight she trades
hibiscus for a last, bitter treat. Her past hovers,

hovers, hovers. Once a blur, tonight she slows. Swallows. Lands
on my doorstep at midnight.

Perfectly still,
as if a cat has mouthed her there.

You are a poppy seed

and already
my body no longer belongs
to me. At night the ancestors

are relentless in my dreams, and the living
suspect you are more
than a flu.

I take three pregnancy tests to be sure
this anxious brain
is not playing tricks.

My breasts are too sore
for my uniform,
and my back is in knots
again, I wake up
crying from pain.

I am afraid
to do anything.

Recall

that the basement
is dark. We are
at Aunty's house and upstairs
it is Christmas.

I am Benadryl heavy
because her house is filled
with cats. Beside me, my cousins

sleep warm on a mattress on the concrete
floor. I wake to a light
at the back of the basement
and go to it.

Uncle is building toys.

He whispers to come and see
what he is doing. I remember
that I liked him
and was afraid of him. I understood
that he loved my cousins
more than me and I
was jealous.

I was outside of many things.

My cousin

looks over the brim
of her chardonnay
and asks what she is afraid
to have answered:

Was my Dad
         one of them?

I look across the hump
of my pregnancy, wish
to swallow this story
with anything other than
useless air.

The only thing I know:

he is dead now. I shrug and say,

Your wine
is getting warm.

An unsharpened knife is
the most dangerous tool

in the kitchen. I unhook
the last family photo
from the wall above the stove, burn sage
over the counters, the knives, the roasting
fork scratched with my uncle's initials
burn out everything
he ever told me about cooking red cabbage
and peeling the shells from prawns. Open

the windows to the rain
and release myself. It is spring
beneath this final crop of snow, and I
have grieved myself

empty. To cook for my family
is to nourish the dead
even as
they devour me.

Gravedig

I. Spade

Ideally a grave is eight feet long, three
wide. It's been said
that six feet is actually a perfect depth,
though others suggest
four and a half. It's true

a shallower depth means
a sexton can easily climb
himself out. But we

are no sextons. We have been made
to dig this hole ourselves.

Let's begin.

Clear the patch
of feather-sage; pocket some
for burning later. On the topsoil, lay
the frame, crafted from old barn walls
and nails procured from the railway line.

Its careful lines
our only guide.
Spade in.

Boot to ground, the blade
will cut a plume
of dust and dry air. Do not
be fooled.

This is the story coating
our mouths and lungs. *Spit it out.*

Add to the gravel pile
your thirty lost first teeth. One
for each grandchild, tucked below
sleep-damp pillows. A visitor
replaced them with quarters
while we slept, dead.

This layer
comes away easiest. Save
your strength.

Our old way

of wandering, how we read
the street signs, crossed
at lights. The reasons we drank
a toast, how we prayed.

Confessions: all things
hidden. The ways
that secrets are true
even if when we never speak
them. Truth

is not the thing
we judge.

Things I will gift you

Unkempt hair
and freckled hands.

A clan
that eats itself crazy.

Orange seed

now, and I
will be a mother
if you stay
where you are supposed to
for thirty-eight weeks.

I am haunted
by Plath's doll grip,
and a different fear that you
might survive.

I don't know
how to bring you
into the arms of this family. I know
what they will whisper
into your ears to keep you
from telling.

I can offer you
sleeplessness,
hard drinking,
chronic scratching, and
binge eating.
The understanding

that lucky ones survive
but live
with shut mouths.

How hushed the nights

of memory. I remember
them as peaceful. So strange,

adult knowing. How knowing
unbraids peace. How
you can never truly
remember.

The thing
we have lost
among others is our word

for a deep and settled sleep. A word for good
memory—the Michif for unforced

sobriety, a word that tells me
I can mother. Shows me

how to speak

these secrets.

How to speak.

I have no business here

I am trapped under
my heavy womb, and I know
I can never be a mother.

Today, you are a sweet pea

and I
am always hungry. Every song
on my morning commute
makes me cry. I eat
saltines and ginger candy —you
spit them back all day long.

My body is strange; I want to sleep
all the time, but when I do
the ancestors haunt, trying
to get a piece of you. I will not let

them, not yet. Today you are not
ready for their stories.

You have only dimples
where your ears will be.

Tonight

I wore my black dress, sash
tied around you, a hard nest
beneath my ribs. It is the mourning
sash, black on red, and I wore it
so you would understand

our sorrows. With gifts
of joy and tribe
come sharpened
teeth and a place to drink
your tears. Tonight

we feast on bison and fry bread
and I read quietly
while the house gets wild
on white wine and sambucca.

I feel you
kick away, pressing
your paws into my inner meat.

These are not the bones

I was born with. I am loose
and boneless. I am

a five-foot earthworm, eating
rivers and causing chasms
with my toothless, open mouth.

Both male and female, I wear
my wet skin. Without my bones
I cannot heal

or walk. I cannot chew.
I can only slither
over this cold ground
rough. I mouth rainwashed
pavement. I know

to mourn now
these bones, arms, teeth
sex organs. A mouth
free of the filthy ground, and skin
that once was rough
and dry and clean.

Now is the time

for burning in. To smudge
the things
I can't remember
and the things I wish
to forget curl up
in the smoke
of sweetgrass, cedar, sage.

I plant them
like tobacco in the garden.
When I look at the stars
I know the grandmothers. I carry

the loosened bones
of the dead in me. They rattle
my baby to sleep.

Please understand

I have lied to you
your entire life.

What's left

of my childhood, of the nicest
men I know? I remember waking warm
to a starred dawn. My cousin,
closest in age, our flannel nightgowns
handed down from older sisters, hands
on the basement window, staring
out to the darkened yard, prints
from her father's boots
pressed into yesterday's snow.

I am the mother

but not
of this place.

My skin
never forgets.

Today, you are a strawberry

and I can no longer
keep down food.

I drink three careful sips of red miso
and hot water, then empty myself

in the public toilet at work. I check
my uniform pants daily for sprays of vomit

that betray our secret. This week,
you wake me from fevered dreams

at four in the morning while your father snores
content beside me. When he reaches

for you in his sleep, I push
his heavy hand away. I do not have room

right now.
Every inch of my skin is used

by you,
and I am unsure where that leaves me:

hungry
yet empty.

One
except   two.

Gravedig

II. Pick Axe

The sod is cut now
and rolled back like a prayer
rug on a clay floor. Set it aside.

When the grave is filled, this will cover
the mess, and no one will know
we were here.

Pick axe.
Arm strength.
Sweat.

We've broken
down all the eye
can see. Remember:

a grave, seven feet deep
can house up to three family members.

We are housing numbers unknown, and so
we must dig. Work
until our palms blister,
seep. Break down
black terra. The axe thumps

on dry topsoil, eats
back the dust. This part is easy,
it requires no speech.
Only patience. A break

for water when our mouths cotton
up. Thirst can redirect
memory, dig past
fishing trips and sleeping bags
on uncarpeted floors. The playhouse

at the garden's edge,
the trampoline. Every Auntie
who braided our hair. Every Uncle
who kissed our face.

Send us your bones

for the other grannies, from my sisters

to build an aviary
for our bodies, they are not
so brittle now
that we could not stand inside them.

Send us your teeth, and let us
bite. Ours are dull and swinging
in our gums. When we open our mouths

they clatter like ice chips.
Send us your skin, lovely
and brown. Give us your blackness

to hide in—it is thicker and darker
than ours, and we need to wear you
like a coat, for we have never been
this cold.

Today, you are a tamarind

ball, sugared. And already
you are kicking. Already
you have hair and your fingers
are sprouting tiny nails. I wake
at night, dreams of you

scratching me from the inside.
Think of my own fingernails, how for years
I have scratched my legs at night, bringing
infection, scabs, scars

over scars. Someday I will
tell you why.

The ones who do not believe

ask why
it is so easy for us—
then take a wafer
on their tongue and pray it
into flesh. There are stranger things

than this: the mystery
of lost teeth, how they became
coins in the night. This truth

was as easy to swallow
as wine

prayed
into blood.

I give you my bones

and you plant them
in a place where there is more sky
than grass. Not here

in the city—here
is not where you will find
our stories.

When I decided to give you
my bones, I pulled them long
and blood-shone from beneath
my oldest skin,

stripped them, chewed them
as a dog's treat at dinner. I did this
for you, so you would never be
boneless. Don't worry

about me. I have swept
cement without my bones. I
do not need them.

These are the empty stories
of our past, cages for you—
like Batoche, Duck Lake—

all the places perhaps
you'll return to. These bones are
splintered,
their marrow sucked. They are
a poor gift.

Do with them
what you must.

I once tried to learn

back our stolen words, the ones thieved
in church and industrial school, spat
upon in legions and alleys
until we too spat
and walked away. I tried

to learn back
the grandmother words, but no matter
how often I spoke them aloud, the grandmothers
were soft and silent.
I never learned. I tried

to scrape these colonies from us, but we
were coated so thickly like years of old paint,

they did not budge. I thought
if I learned the names
of our kin, I could hand you
this land and you
could wear your place here
like a woolen shawl.

Instead what I gifted
was *la penn n'dayaan,* too heavy
my sorrow.

You are the end

of this family. It's not
your fault. I just think
if I were single, or
childless I could still return.

Drink my way
through these truths. Perhaps

I would have kept
the family secrets the way
I was taught to. But now
I imagine you running, as I did
room to room
bare legged and laughing, falling
asleep in the basement
in a pile of your cousins.

I must never give you
all I had.

New year's

amid the fall of spark and colour
we snake from our skin,
tongue-pink and pearled.
Only on this night—the old
days shaken and hung. Particles

of dust linger in a streak
of sunlight. Suck bruises
into each other's mouths, fuck
like strangers and fall

into the bloom
of cool white sheets. Sleep drunk
and half-dressed.

We are the same
old stories.

We are the dream

US election 2016, after Langston Hughes

deferred.
We did not explode.
At the tail-end of the battle, we failed
to recognize
there was price
to be paid
for this pride. We

are the dream.
We lowered our fists
when our biceps ached,
and took it on the jaw
and handed back
our fate.

Misfits of a war, we failed
to see the festering that pulsed
beneath our scars.

What do I know of this mother tongue?

What good is *duck,*
river, shore,
and *sky?*

The name
in Cree for the town
where I was born. But not
betrayal, hypocrisy,
disillusion. I was not gifted

words for *coping*
or *losing,* and I cannot
teach them

to this belly-cub,
say to her

Look up
to the stars, they are your people.

I can only say
in English

That is the sky and
We are alone.

My mother always tells me

to speak
to the dead. She says

You have always trusted them
more than us, so listen. But how
can I trust the ones who know our paths,
when they have seen
every sin?

If I am the first

of your ancestral line.

Mine is a story
short and unspirited,

You will not be haunted, but
you are safe.

Slow loss

you have fingerprints,
your first swirls
of independence. This is the moment

we separate. Already
I can feel myself
losing you.

Today, you are a Julie mango

—soft,
sweet, and
easily bruised.

The midwife confirms
you've been pulling
the umbilical cord,
waking me with sharp pains
at night. I imagine

you swinging around
while I toss.
She tells me you can hear
my voice now.

I am not ready.

My husband sits through the funeral
of a nine-year-old boy

He is not a man of faith, but
a friend. He sits
in the Orthodox church in his work jeans and studies
the coffin. Texts me from the reception:
sad, babe. So fucking sad.
I could not be with him

in his grief. I am not a friend, I am
soon to be a mother, can't watch
a child be buried.

I leave him to his peers,
his child is safe with me.

I hope

you will have
a life so kind

that you'll never
write poetry.

Now, you are a girl

and I think of the years
you will ruin
your future, as I did
many times. Already

you keep me awake
kicking and punching,
no thought
of what your actions
do to me. I've been taking beatings

my whole life yet
I have never held anyone
as long as I have carried you. No one

has heard my blood
or ridden the movement
of my lungs. No one

has had the courage
to take refuge
in my flesh.

Except now

you are a daughter, no longer
a cherry, poppyseed,
a ripe Julie mango, but a daughter
with limb on limbs and all
the soft and sacred parts. Yours

is the skin and the bones
I have grown from fat
and blood. As my body
makes room for your girlhood
I shove
familial fear aside.

Beneath my lungs you toss
my guts off like a hot blanket in the night.
All the places I used to eat, breathe, make waste—
they are all you now.

I am just the thing
that carries you.

Meaning, star

I named you
for the stars so you'll never be
lonesome. I was told long ago
that the stars are the place
of our grandmothers, the ones who know
the story's ending

Trust them if you can.
I cannot

protect you
from my rough past. Instead

I am gifting you
my wolverine's

hide, daggered claws, teeth.
I named you for the stars

because land is
unkind
and the grandmothers
fell quiet when we needed them
screaming.

Gravedig

III. Backfill

Finally.

Remove the careful frame, kick off
our mud-heavy boots. Release

clenched toes. Wiggle. Split
a well-earned root beer. Swallow
it slowly, passed from mouth
to mouth. We are, after all,
still family. We remember

Sundays at the drive-thru
with our uncles in the car. How they crept
up behind us snickering, and squished
ice-cream
cones into our faces
while we licked, then cried.

They were not cruel men, but
mischievous. *This is important.*
Had they been cruel, we'd have less
of a story. Had they been
cruel, the others
would have spoken. No,

they were not cruel. Theirs is a sin
of affection. The reason we
came here. To put back.

Backfill.
This is the favour we do
for our kin. *A grave*
seven feet deep can house
up to three family members. We

are housing
numbers unknown.

We offer the holidays. Games of touch
tag yelping across Diefenbaker Park. Geese
nipping bread from our hands. Sleepovers
when we woke in the night. Mornings
when our cousins were quieter

than they'd been the night
before. There is room
enough for every embrace, some memories
are really as good as they seemed. The men
who rubbed our bellies
when we had the stomach flu. Tossed
us in the backyard
swimming pool in our street clothes. They did not

always smell of beer. To the grave,
we offer the bad and hold on to the good. We offer
our guilt, because all of us knew. We no longer
offer our children.

Burn the sage.

We're done.

Remember

the unpaved roads
of our early days,
taken always with reckless speed.
The soundtrack of little girls

screeching along the gravel.
These roads, where we clung
to the truck's blue bed,
braced only with warnings about school
children bucked onto the backroad,

their teeth and bones scattered
like crickets on asphalt. These, the risks of too-young
parents. Now, the days of new parenthood:
horror stories float up

during the dark silence of midnight feeds
as we stare at the mooned head of a newborn and think
How easily lost.

Forgive them, our parents, just a little.
In our sleeplessness, think perhaps the job they did
was not so bad. We have not yet begun to peel our skin
from its fat cap, remove the blood-heavy

blankets of our youth.
We have not yet learned
to fail.

On changing my name

A woman approaching her mid-day break taps her finger
on the same line I've signed twice:
"Your new name, hun. You keep signing *Morgan*."

I apologize. Stiffly
write the name I will share with my daughter,
linked to my first initial. Act like I've been practising it
all the months between first date and marriage. Consider
dotting the i's
with hearts, then disregard.

Awkward and messy on the line, the early
cursive lessons of grade school. My hand longs
for the series of lines and dots that guided
my sharpened pencils this lifetime past. I wish
for familiar tools: index finger and thumb,
an inky pen,
the bones of my wrist, fresh white paper.

Instead I have a dry ballpoint and a government
form. In this one act, I am a new
woman, one who buys groceries, swaps
the toilet roll, who will rise at five
to breastfeed, wipe puke from her clothing,
change diapers while her husband
snores below the soft duvet.

The woman eyes the clock
takes the form,
stamps it soundly.

Halfway

Your tiny girl-paws stretch
inside me. Soon

you will outgrow me. Soon
the world will crab in and claw

you from me. I long for relief—
from this taste of vomit

mixed with constant hunger, your game
of crave, then purge, then crave.

For you, I spend my days
crouched and retching.

Last night, I dreamt

I pushed you out onto the sheets
of an old motel bed. My mother

was your midwife, and we birthed
you into the place where she

had pushed me out all those years ago.
You emerged silent, and when

I held you, you were a pointy-eared
imp, all folded skin and black eyes. My mother

said I had to wash the after-birth
from your soap-white skin

and draw you a bath
in a plastic basin. I did not want her

to hold you, so I folded my fingers around
you, small as a piglet but far more still.

I dipped you, cup-sized,
into the water, and slowly

you came apart in my hands.

I woke up screaming.

Already

you are blessed. Tonight

Gregory Scofield kissed
his fingertips, pressed
them to my belly, he said

you were a sacred thing.
All of the sage-burned
words are yours.

You
blessed thing.

Your bones

are footprints in snow. I remember
growing each one
in my anxious womb. How you
pressed the soles
of your feet between my ribs and how I

gingerly pushed you aside to make room
for my lungs. How after each breath
you clawed your way back
as if to say
This place is mine.

One week today, I am
a mother. My husband,
a father. The space between us
is populated by nursing pillows
a sliced abdomen, breasts
that throb and leak—and you,
the thing we both want nearest.

We have not yet learned
to share you.

Midnight feeding

where you nurse me thirsty, then fall
dreamily from my nipple. I feel
my body weeping—six days
of motherhood. I wear the stains
of my new role on the front
of my shirt, no matter
how often you latch there.

These breasts have been useless
my entire life, in fact, I have hated them.
And now they are the most
swollen and painful parts
of me, and the thing
you look for the most. The bridge

between what we were
and are. We share
our skin
and this strange milk.

This is the stillness

I watch your fontanelle, stare myself fuzzy
to find the rise of your bird chest. Pull out
of a parking spot and panic, certain I have left you
on the front stoop, even as you sleep,

coo from the back seat.

At home I cling you to me, thinking
of how I have lost every trust, thinking
that a woman with a family such as this
cannot keep safe
something so fragile. Thinking
how the ancestors are fringing
every moment of my mothering now.

When we are alone, you stare
past me and smile broadly at walls
and ceilings and window blinds
as I shoo away *jumbies,* their hot mischief.

Stella, don't talk to them, look away!
I say. But you see them anyway
and laugh wildly.

Knead for ten minutes

Her hands are freckled and pale, paler
from a dusting of flour on skin, countertop
shirt front. I am watching, again

learning her legacy
after thirty years of failure. She begins
with a thick mug of warm water—

not hot, as warm as the baby's bath. White
sugar from habit, but molasses
would be fine. She blooms

two packets of yeast, adds water
to wheat flour, a tablespoon
of canola oil and a half-palm of salt.

The yeast foams, smells of good ale
and though she doesn't drink beer, that's how she knows
it's ready. These days she uses a dough hook

to start, but I remember her hands
pulling flour into water like a river
current gathering sand. She stands

aside, demands I press my fingers into the hooked dough
to feel its warmth, how it springs
under my touch. *You'll always remember how it feels.*

I turn everything out onto my bleached and floured counter.
Knead, she says. *For ten minutes exactly.*

No less, no more.
This is the secret to perfect bread:
time.

She puts the dough into a large, oiled bowl
and covers it with plastic wrap, placing
it on the stovetop. As a girl I remember

how she would find a square of sunlight
and set the bowl on the floor in it
if the house was cold.

We talk about the baby, sleeping in a swing. We talk
about the family, and she cries for what we lost.
I tell her that most of what I remember

is no longer good. I tell her everything
that was told to me and by who. She weeps
for the good only
she can recall. We fold laundry:

first the towels, tea towels, the knitted
dishcloths her mother made each year and rolled
into our Christmas stockings. She talks

about how I would sit on the counter
watching her make the bread in the mornings
when my sisters had gone to school. How I loved

to eat raw dough, so much that I would give myself
a stomachache. She remembers trying to teach me
to make bread as a teenager. How, frustrated, I stomped

from the kitchen and refused to come back. The secret
was time, and I was too wild to wait.

When the dough has doubled in size, she oils the countertop
and turns it out again, kneading slowly. Then lets it rest
ten minutes more before slicing it in quarters.

She demonstrates how to loaf
each one, rolling it to seal the bottom. Narrates
each step. My daughter

sleeps soundly and I limp around, the incision
from her delivery tugging my old skin.
My mother puts the loafs in her mother's glass pans, slides

them into the oven. Forty-five minutes, she says. We make
the beds, clean the coffee table, talk about the baby, who wakes
in her swing to bat at a rattle hanging above her head.

When the timer goes, my mother brushes cold butter
on the tops of the loaves and then slices a piece, handing it to me.
This is her oldest story.

Building a nest from these bones

The day she was born, I wanted to scream
her alive, teach her the war cries
of our women. Instead,

the doctor sliced her silently from me and emptied
me without feeling. Held her a sweeping moment
above me—*Here is your daughter*—then pulled her back

before I could raise
my dopey eyes to nothing more than the blue
drape and two spots of fresh blood.

My daughter cried out, screamed
herself into my silence, and I felt
the old bones clatter around

my paralyzed limbs. I gathered
them tight to build her a place
where she could scream herself wild,

where no one would touch her,
where the ghosts would not enter. In this nest,
her new bones will grow.

ACKNOWLEDGMENTS

Early versions of some of the poems in this collection have appeared in *Hamilton Arts & Letters, Poetry Is Dead,* and the anthology *Release Any Words Stuck Inside of You: Untethered Collection of Shorts* (Applebeard Editions).

Maarsii to my editors Leigh Nash and Adebe DeRango-Adem for being my steadfast navigators on this journey. And to Norm Nehmetallah and Invisible Publishing for championing this work with such warmth and support.

Maarsii to my sisters, Alanna and Jacqueline Morgan, who supported the writing of this collection even while walking their own healing paths. We are the three parts of a good, strong braid.

For my husband, Sean, who found himself in a story he did not expect. Thank you for soaking my tears up with your shoulders and reminding me that good love is good medicine.

And for Stella, who slept so well draped over my shoulder and who nursed while I pecked out these poems with one hand. You are my greatest joy.

To Mavis and Earle Morgan, who heard and who believed. I am so grateful.

To my family, the living and the dead: it is not always easy, but it is always love. I hope you'll someday understand.

And last, to my mother. Thank you for teaching me in your own way to take a punch, to speak my truth, and to scream when the world wants me to be quiet. I know I am not an easy daughter.

Maarsii, thank you.

Cara-Lyn Morgan comes from both Indigenous (Métis) and Immigrant (Trinidadian) roots in the place known as Turtle Island and Canada. She was born in Oskana, known now as Regina, Saskatchewan, and lives, works, and gardens, in the traditional territories of the Anishinaabeg, Haudenosaunee, Huron-Wendat, and Mississaugas of the Credit peoples. Her debut collection of poetry, *What Became My Grieving Ceremony*, won the 2015 Fred Cogswell Award for Poetic Excellence. Her second collection, *Cartograph*, explores healing, cultural duality, and colonization.

INVISIBLE PUBLISHING produces fine Canadian literature for those who enjoy such things. As an independent, not-for-profit publisher, we work to build communities that sustain and encourage engaging, literary, and current writing.

Invisible Publishing has been in operation for over a decade. We released our first fiction titles in the spring of 2007, and our catalogue has come to include works of graphic fiction and nonfiction, pop culture biographies, experimental poetry, and prose.

We are committed to publishing writers with diverse perspectives. In acknowledging historical and systemic barriers, and the limits of our existing catalogue, we emphatically encourage writers from LGBTQ2SIA+ communities, Indigenous writers, and writers of colour to submit their work.

Invisible Publishing is also home to the Bibliophonic series of music books and the Throwback series of CanLit reissues.

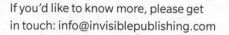
If you'd like to know more, please get in touch: info@invisiblepublishing.com